PRAYERS FOR TODAY

FRANK COLQUHOUN is a former Canon Residentiary and Vice-Dean of Norwich Cathedral. Previously, most of his life was spent in South London, where he was for seven years Vicar of Wallington and subsequently Canon and Chancellor of Southwark Cathedral and Principal of the Southwark Ordination Course. Now retired, he lives at Bexhill in Sussex.

His many books include *Parish Prayers*, *Contemporary Parish Prayers* and *New Parish Prayers*. He is also editor of the revised edition of the BBC service book, *New Every Morning*. His previous publications for Triangle were *Prayers that Live* and *Family Prayers*.

D0674776

PRAYERS
FOR TODAY

Compiled and edited by

FRANK COLQUHOUN

First published 1989
Triangle
SPCK
Holy Trinity Church
Marylebone Road
London NW1 4DU

Fifth impression 1992

British Library Cataloguing in Publication Data

Colquhoun, Frank
  Prayers for today.
  1. Christian life. Prayer, Devotional works
  I. Title
  242'.8

  ISBN 0-281-04403-1

Typeset by Inforum Ltd, Portsmouth
Printed in Great Britain by
BPCC Hazells Ltd
Member of BPCC Ltd

CONTENTS

PREFACE

As the title indicates, this short book of prayers is intended to have a modern ring about it and deal with contemporary issues.

It is divided into three sections. The first is primarily concerned with the things of everyday life and the prayers are largely of a personal character: not the sort of prayers for use in public worship.

The second section is occupied with the spiritual side of life, the life of the Christian pilgrim in its various aspects. In actual life of course the secular and the spiritual cannot be separated, but in a book like this it has to be done to facilitate reference.

In the third section, 'The world we live in', a wider range of subjects is explored. Here the prayers are less personal and the language more conventional, suitable for use in church if desired.

More than half the prayers are my own, the great majority having been written for this book. To such prayers no ascription of authorship has been added. Prayers designated 'Adapted' have been derived from various sources and considerably modified or rewritten. An asterisk (*) after an ascription indicates that some of the original wording has been altered or shortened.

Prayers for Today is my third Triangle book. Its publication gives me the opportunity of paying a personal tribute to Miss Myrtle Powley as the originator and editor of this enterprising paperback imprint. I also wish to thank her for her friendship and the generous help she has given me over the years.

FRANK COLQUHOUN

PART ONE

The Life of Everyday

PRAYERS FOR TODAY

1

OURSELVES

My Life

1

'*What is your life?*' asks the Bible writer (James 4.14).

It is the life, Lord, which you yourself have given me:

the outer life of my body, with its physical powers and faculties;

the inner life of my soul, with its capacity to understand and reason, to feel and to will;

the higher life of my spirit, by which I know you, commune with you, worship and adore you, my God and my King.

Life's Purpose

2

Lord, our life is not meaningless.

You have shown us what we are in the world for:

not for ourselves but for others;

not to get what we can but to give what we can;

not to make a name for ourselves but to glorify your name;

not just to live and die but to die to sin and live for Christ.

Help us to acknowledge these things, and may our lives not miss the purpose for which you made them.

Lord, I believe there is something you want me to do 3
with my life.

Help me to find out what it is.

Help me by your grace to do it.

And help me to the end of my days to carry out your plan and purpose and to live for your glory.

My Father, thank you for knowing me better than I know myself.

Thank you for letting me know myself better than others know me.

Make me better than they suppose I am, and forgive me for what they do not know. For Jesus Christ's sake.

Based on an Islamic prayer

5

Lord God, I recognise the truth of the saying that 'I am not what I think I am, but what I *think*, I am.'

My thoughts shape my character and personality and determine what I say and do.

By your grace then I will guard my thoughts and drive out the false and evil ones by letting in those that are true and good.

So may I be the person *you* want me to be, and not what I think I am.

My body 6

Lord, your word teaches me that as a Christian my body is the temple of the Holy Spirit and belongs to you.

Help me therefore to honour and care for my body:
    to guard my health and keep as fit as possible;
    to control my impulses and appetites;
    and in all things to be chaste and temperate.

By your grace may I glorify you both in body and soul, through the power of the Spirit of Jesus Christ.

Our Father, as we thank you for the gift of life, we thank you also for the faculties which enable us to enjoy it:
    our eyes to see the wonders of your world,
    our ears to hear speech and the sound of music,
    our lips with which to talk and sing,
    our hands for working and our feet for walking.
    Make us daily grateful for all your gifts and help us to use them all for your glory.

Our character 8

Our Father, help us to remember that what we are matters more than what we do, and that our character is the only thing we shall take out of this world when we die.
    Make us the sort of people you want us to be.
    Direct our thoughts, our interests, our ambitions, that we may build a sound Christian character on the foundations of love, kindness, honesty, truthfulness and faith; that apart from our words and actions, what we are may be a witness to him whom we love and serve, Jesus Christ our Lord.

For courage 9

Lord God, set us free from the spirit of fear, especially the fear of other people, and give us the grace of courage:
    courage to get up when we are down;
    courage to own up when we are wrong;
    courage to bear up when we are weary;
    and at all times courage to stand up for Jesus, our Saviour and our Lord.

For honesty

Lord, when so much of the world's business is dominated by corruption and double dealing, we ask you for the virtue of honesty:
   honesty in our dealings with one another;
   honesty in all our financial affairs;
   honesty in admitting our mistakes;
   honesty in keeping our promises.
   Give us the joy of facing the world with a clear conscience, honest with ourselves, with others, and above all with you, our God and King.

For cheerfulness

Lord Christ, give us the grace of cheerfulness – not a bogus, artificial sort but something real:
   a cheerful spirit deep down within us;
   a cheerful countenance with which to face the world;
   a cheerful attitude to life with all its troubles.
   May we never dispense gloom and despondency to others but impart hope and faith and gladness; and may we ourselves meet all life's ills in the same spirit, by your grace and goodness.

For purity

It is the pure in heart, Jesus said, who are blessed of you, our God.
   We long that this blessing may be ours!
   For if our hearts are pure, so also will be our thoughts, our imaginations, our motives, our loves, our lives.
   Keep us, O Lord, untainted from the corruption of the world, and make us remember:
      Blest are the pure in heart,
      for they shall see our God.

Lord God, our hearts and lives are open to you and you know us better than we know ourselves.

Keep us from seeming to be what we are not;
from having a name we do not live up to;
from all pretence and deceit.

Make us sincere in our religious life, our home life, our friendships and our personal relationships.

Give us the satisfaction of making our way in the world with clean hands and a clear conscience; and save us, O Lord, from the snare of a double mind.

Our speech 14

Set a guard, O Lord, on my mouth:
and keep the door of my lips. (Psalm 141.3)
Father, let us each make that prayer our own.

Save us from foolish or hurtful talk, from speaking lies or making false promises.

Give us the courage to say what we mean, and the honesty to mean what we say.

And may no words of ours be displeasing to you but carry your blessing; through Jesus Christ our Lord.

Memory 15

We thank you, our Father, for the gift of memory
by which we live again the past
and recall old friends and bygone days
with joy and gratitude.
But we thank you still more for the power to forget,
so that the wounds and slights we have suffered
can hurt us no more,
and our own mistakes and misdeeds
may be buried in oblivion and no longer condemn.

Derived from *Two Gifts* by Margaret Hancock

Lord, we do not ask to be clever, but we do ask for a share of plain common sense.

Give us insight into the ways of the world, understanding of people, and perception of what is true and false, so that we do not harm ourselves or others by making foolish mistakes.

Yes, Lord, please give us common sense.

Or else just sense.

Humour 17

'You must be joking!' When they say that to me, Lord, perhaps I am. And why not?

Life is not a joke but a joke is part of life; for when you created man you implanted in him a sense of humour.

Without that gift our days would be drab, solemn and cheerless.

But in your mercy we have the capacity to see the funny side of life, to laugh as well as to cry, and to laugh at ourselves, even when things go wrong.

What a blessing you have made us like this!

Lord, we thank you.

The fools 18

Fools say to themselves, 'There is no God'.   (Psalm 14.1)

How strange, Lord, that people should talk such folly!

The more I see of the beauty, variety and order of the world about me, and think about the miracle of creation, the more I am inclined to fall on my knees and worship the Creator.

Yet there are still some who say there is no God.

Lord, I may be a bit of a fool, but I am not as big a fool as that.

2

THROUGH THE DAY

In the morning 19

Thank you, our Father, for another night of quiet sleep
and rest.

Thank you for renewed health and energy as we start
out on another day.

Thank you for the certainty that, whatever the day may
hold, we do not face it alone but with a Friend beside us
who will never let us down.

O God, help me this day 20
to use the brains you have given me
without pride,
the hands you have given me
without sloth,
and the tongue you have given me
without malice;
for Jesus Christ's sake.

Stanley Pritchard

This day 21

This is the day that the Lord has made;
Let us rejoice and be glad in it. (Psalm 118.24)

Today is your new gift to me, Lord;
I thank you for it.
Today may have its special difficulties;
I will face them with a brave heart.
Today will never come again;
I pray for grace to make the best use of it.

Lord, our greatest joys are not those which money can buy
but the good gifts that surround us in our daily lives:

    the sun that warms us and brightens our days;
    the countryside in all its matchless beauty;
    the gardens with their flowers and fruits;
    our homes and families and friends;
    our health of body and soundness of mind;
    our books and hobbies and music.

Father, for these and all your blessings which give us joy
we give you thanks and praise.

'Thanks' and 'Yes' 23

> *For all that has been – 'Thanks!'*
> *For all that shall be – 'Yes!'*

> (Dag Hammarskjold)

Lord, help us to adopt this same positive attitude to life: to
express our gratitude for the past and affirm our faith for
the future.

You have poured so many blessings upon us that as we
look back over the years we can only say, again and again,
'Thanks!'

And as we face the unknown days ahead, may we do so
in a spirit of trust, accepting whatever is to come with a
fearless 'Yes!'

The living Christ still has two hands, one to point the way, the other held out to help us along. (T.W. Mason)

Lord Christ, we need both your hands as we journey through the world:
  your guiding hand to direct us, for we are ignorant of the road ahead and dare not rely on our own wisdom;
  and your helping hand to support us, for the going is hard and we may stumble and fall.
  Be near us all through our journey and lead us safely home.

The weather   25

Heavenly Father, because we depend so much on the weather for so many things in life, we thank you for the great variety of weather which we experience in the course of the year.
  For sunshine and rain, clouds and wind, snow and frost, we praise and magnify you, Creator and Lord of all.

The rain   26

Lord, how often we complain about wet weather, without realising how stupid and ungrateful we are.
  For rain is one of your most precious gifts. People of other lands know that better than we do.
  It is the rain that waters the earth and makes it fertile and fruitful and saves us from famine.
  It is the rain that supplies our drinking water and saves us from drought.
  What a blessing it is, Lord, that the ordering of the climate is in your hands, not ours!
  Thank you for the rain, and for all your mercy towards us.

The unexpected

Lord, keep us aware that our daily life may not always run
the same smooth course.
Something unexpected may change the pattern of our
day, even of our life.
It may be something that happens at home.
It may be something to do with our work.
It may be a surprising bit of news.
It may be a sudden accident or illness.
It may be any number of things.
We do not know what a day may bring.
How can we prepare for life's sudden demands? In one
way only: by committing each day into your hands and
trusting you for whatever is to come.

The day's end

Father, the day is over and at its end we do three things:
we thank you for the blessings of the day that is gone;
we commit ourselves, our families and loved ones to
your care and protection for the night;
and we pray for those known to us who are in special
need.
We do these things in the name of Christ our Lord.

The gift of sleep

Merciful Father, at the end of the day we ask you to put
away from us worry and every anxious fear; that committing our tasks, ourselves, and all we love into your
keeping, we may, now that night draws on, receive from
you the precious gift of sleep, and when morning breaks go
forth with grateful hearts to serve you through another
day, in the name of our Lord Jesus Christ.

Anglican Church of Canada*

Lord, as we lie down to sleep in the darkness of the night, drive from our souls the darkness of fear and anxiety and troubled thoughts.

Give us your peace and bring us safely through the darkness to the light of a new day; through Jesus Christ our Lord.

3

WORK AND LEISURE

Daily work

Father, we accept that work is one of your gifts to us, to be undertaken with gratitude.

Help us to bring to it the best we have to offer and to find satisfaction in work well done.

As we remember the example of our Lord who served in the carpenter's shop at Nazareth, may we regard no work as common or mean; and may we do everything as in your sight and for your praise, not for the praise of men.

God our Father, thank you for calling us to serve you in our daily occupations.

Help us cheerfully to obey this calling in the places where we work, in our homes, and in our society.

And make us always ready to seize opportunities of doing good to others and helping those in need; through Jesus Christ our Lord.

Basil Naylor*

Forth in thy name, O Lord, I go,
    My daily labour to pursue;
Thee, only thee, resolved to know,
    In all I think or speak or do.

The work thy wisdom hath assigned
    O let me cheerfully fulfil;
In all my works thy presence find,
    And prove thy good and perfect will.

Charles Wesley

Hands

Lord Christ, in your days on earth your hands were constantly stretched out to heal and serve and bless.

We have hands similar to yours.

What marvellous pieces of mechanism they are!

What an endless variety of things they can do!

Throughout the day, from morning to night, we use them for a hundred different purposes, without even thinking of them, still less thanking you for them.

We pray that as our hands serve us so well, they may also be of service to others; and so we sing:

> *Take my hands, and let them move*
> *At the impulse of thy love.*

Our service of others

Heavenly Father, teach us again and again that the world is not a pleasure ground for our own enjoyment but a field of service for the benefit of others.

Give us eyes of compassion for the suffering and afflicted around us; save us from neglecting any opportunity of giving help; and when we come face to face with human need, may we never pass by on the other side.

Those who serve us

Our Father, we remember before you those who serve us in the everyday ministries of life:

doctors, dentists, nurses, teachers;
assistants in shops, banks and offices;
builders, plumbers, mechanics;
milkmen, postmen, dustmen.

Keep us mindful, O Lord, of what they and others do for us, and may we accept their services with gratitude in Christ's name.

There is a time for everything under the sun, said the wise Preacher (Ecclesiastes 3.1).

In the pattern of our life there is not only a time to work but also a time to rest.

Lord, help us to remember this and to recognise that leisure times are as important and necessary as any others.

So we ask your blessing on our holidays, hobbies and recreations; our social activities and our relaxed hours at home; that in doing us good they may equip us better for our daily work and duties.

Relaxation 38

We are so desperately busy and there is so much to be done that we have no time for relaxation.

So, Lord, we often think.

Teach us to think again and to remember that our minds and bodies need a break from work at times if we are to be at our best.

Teach us to find relaxation in books and music, in our hobbies and pleasures, in our weekends and holidays, in our home life, church life and social life.

And let us remember that we relax not to become lazy but to enable us to work harder. And all for your glory.

Books 39

Lord, what a relief it is when we are tired and exhausted to relax with a book! A book which will lift us out of the harsh realities of life into a world of fantasy and imagination.

We thank you for books that help us in this way –

novels, romances, mysteries – and for those who have written them for our pleasure.

To read only such books would be a tragedy. To ignore them completely might be a mistake.

Lord, give us sense and discrimination in what we read.

Holidays 40

Heavenly Father, we thank you for the times of rest and relaxation which are given to us in the course of our lives.

Teach us to use our leisure and our holidays to rebuild our bodies and renew our minds; and may we be strengthened and refreshed in spirit for our daily work and the service of your kingdom; through Jesus Christ our Lord.

Episcopal Church in the USA

Music 41

Thank you, Father, for the gift of music through which we can express the varying moods of life: joy and delight, melancholy and sadness, wonder and worship, love and devotion.

Thank you for the power of music to relax our minds and lift our spirits.

And thank you that, like the psalmist of old, we too can make a joyful noise to you in music and song; through Jesus Christ our Lord.

Adapted from a prayer by Patricia Mitchell

Laughter 42

Lord, how glorious and infectious laughter can be!

Not the hollow laughter of the fool, or the humourless

17

laughter of the snob, but the genuine, spontaneous laughter invoked by the things we see and hear and talk about.

Thank you, Lord, for the gift of laughter.

And as life goes on, give us plenty of fresh things to laugh at, and save us from taking ourselves too seriously.

Preparing for retirement 43

Heavenly Father, we pray for those whose working days are coming to an end and who are now facing retirement.

Prepare them in mind and spirit for this traumatic change in their life's pattern.

Grant that their future days and years may be positive and creative, beneficial not only to themselves but to their families and friends; and may they open up fresh avenues of service in their church and community; for the sake of Jesus Christ our Lord.

Based on a prayer by Michael Botting

Times of change 44

Lord, life changes and so must we.

Save us from getting set in our ways.

Make us open-minded, and help us to overcome our inbuilt prejudices.

May we cheerfully welcome new ideas and enter without fear into new experiences and new patterns of work.

Life changes. We change. But you, O Lord, are eternally the same, and so is your love and care for us.

Glory to your name!

Our Father, as we wonder about the future and what it holds in store, teach us to be neither anxious nor thoughtless.

Not anxious, because we know that our times are in your hands and that you will guide our way through life step by step.

And not thoughtless, because as we face the unknown we must use the brains you have given us and exercise our judgment as best we can.

Come what may, in all our future days may your will be done.

MARRIAGE AND THE FAMILY

Christian marriage 46

Dear Lord and Father of mankind,
we thank you for the ordinance of marriage
by which man and woman find fulfilment
in their love for one another.
Bless all Christian husbands and wives.
May your presence enrich their love
and direct their way in life;
and keep them close to each other
in both good times and bad;
through Jesus Christ our Lord.

                                        Adapted

Man and wife 47

Heavenly Father, marriage is of your making. It is you
who have joined us together as man and wife.

Therefore we pray that throughout our married life you
will give us grace at all times
   to be true to one another,
   to consider one another's needs,
   to support one another in trouble,
   to forgive one another's mistakes,
   to love one another to the end.
So may we as man and wife enjoy your constant blessing
and live together for your glory.

Father, save us from being so rushed and busy in our married life that we have few opportunities to enjoy each other as man and wife.

Show us how to make time to be together and do things together; and may we always find our deepest happiness in one another's company; for your love's sake.

Married life

Lord, we know that to many, married life is just something to read about, or talk about, or even to joke about.

To us it is a sacred bond, our chosen path in life.

That path is not always easy. We need grace to persevere in difficult times.

Teach us to practise the old-fashioned virtues of courtesy and consideration, gentleness and kindness; to be unselfish, understanding, and forgiving; and always to put each other first.

And may the blessing we asked of you on our wedding day continue to rest upon us unbroken till the end of our married life; for your name's sake.

Marriage under threat

Heavenly Father, we pray for those whose marriage is losing the love and joy that once was theirs.

Awaken in them the desire to overcome the problems and difficulties that face them.

And grant that through the grace of the Lord Jesus Christ they may rediscover their love for one another and grow together again, through Jesus Christ our Lord.

Diocese of Waiapu, New Zealand

Our Father, some of us know well the joys and trials of
parenthood and what it involves.

But whether or not we know it personally, we pray for
parents with a growing family.

When things go well, make them grateful and give them
gladness of heart; and in difficult times give them strength
and patience to persevere; through Christ our Lord.

Adapted

Our children 52

Our Father, we thank you for the children you have given
us.

We pray for their spiritual development, that they may
grow up

in the fear of God,
in the faith of Christ,
and in the fellowship of the Church,

to love and serve you all their days.

53

Heavenly Father, grant to our children this gift above all,
that as they grow in years they may grow also in the grace
of our Lord Jesus Christ; so that when the time comes they
may go out into the life of the world strong in the faith of
the Lord their God.

Source unknown

A child's birthday

Heavenly Father, the birth of your Son Jesus Christ
brought great joy to Mary and Joseph.
　We thank you for our child ———— whose birthday we
joyfully celebrate today.
　Bless [him] now and in all the years to come; and may
[he] grow up healthy in body and strong in spirit, through
the grace of our Lord Jesus Christ.

Adapted

Young people

Lord of all life, we pray for the young people growing up in
our families, that as they begin to discover something of
themselves and of your world, their gifts and talents may
be used creatively, their decisions may be based on what is
good and of real worth, and their lives may be directed in
the paths you have planned.
　Grant it for the honour of Jesus our Lord.

Adapted

Our home

Most gracious Father,
this is our home:
let your peace rest upon it.
　Let love abide here,
　love of one another,
　love of mankind,
　love of life itself,
　and love of God.
Let us remember that
as many hands build a house,
so many hearts make a home.

Bishop Hugh Blackburne

Lord, though we may not often give thanks before our meals, grant that we may always be grateful:

> grateful for the food we eat and enjoy,
> grateful for the food which comes from other countries,
> and grateful to those who prepare it for our table.

Thank you, God, for everything, in Jesus' name.

Friendship 58

We thank you, our Father, for the circle of friends you have given us: those we know so well and who understand us best and on whom we can always rely.

May that circle not be a narrow one.

As life goes on, help us to enlarge it and bring others inside it, so that both they and we may be enriched by our friendship and be better fitted for life's work and duties.

May the God of love 59
who is the source of all our affection
for each other formed here on earth
take our friendships into his keeping,
that they may continue and increase
throughout life and beyond it,
in Jesus Christ our Lord.

William Temple

5

MONEY AND POSSESSIONS

Possessions 60

A person's true life is not made up of the things he owns.
(Luke 12.13)

Lord Jesus, how hard it is for us to accept that teaching in
a materialistic age, when a person's worth is measured not
by what he is but by what he has.

Help us to get our sense of values right and to view our
temporal possessions in the light of eternity.

You told the story of the rich farmer whose barns were
full but whose soul was empty and who died a spiritual
pauper.

God called that man a fool. Perhaps we ought to ask
ourselves what he thinks of *us*.

61

Heavenly Father, save me from letting my possessions
become the centre of my thinking and so of crowding you
out of my life.

Free me from worry and from becoming obsessed with
the things of transient value.

Enable me to give you the priority in all things and to
seek first your kingdom, knowing that you will provide for
all my daily needs.

Bible Society*

We confess, O Lord, that money often has too big a place in our lives and causes us anxiety about how we should use it.

Help us to get a balanced view of our money and consider, in your presence:

how much we should *spend* on our own normal needs and expenses;

how much we should *save* to provide for our future;

how much we should *give* to others and to charities for the furtherance of your kingdom.

May we constantly remember that our money is something that we hold in trust from you, to be used now while the opportunity is ours. And that we cannot take it with us when we die.

From greed and avarice,　　　　　　　　　　　　　**63**
from selfishness in getting and spending,
from meanness and miserliness,
　　deliver us, good Lord.
And in using the money we have
　help us to spend wisely,
　to give generously,
　to live unselfishly,
thinking always of the needs of others;
　for Jesus Christ's sake.

　　　　　　　　　　　　　　　　　　Source unknown

　　　　　　　　　　　　　　　　　　　　　64

Lord God, in your love you have bestowed upon us gifts such as our forefathers never knew or dreamed of.

Save us from being so occupied with material things that we forget the things which are spiritual; lest having gained the whole world, we lose our own soul; for your mercy's sake.

　　　　　　　　　　　　　　　　　　Daily Prayer

(When the evangelist D.L. Moody came to Britain in the last century, he was asked if he would do something for the miserably poor. 'Yes,' he said, 'and I hope also to do something for the miserably rich.')

Lord, in these prosperous times many are unhappy, not because they have too little but because they have too much.

They have too much of this world's goods, too little of the things of spiritual value.

In the eyes of men they are wealthy; in your eyes they are bankrupt.

Their purses are full but their souls are empty.

Give them, O Lord, and give us all, a proper sense of values and a right understanding of the worth and worthlessness of money in the light of the world to come.

Stewardship 66

Make us ever eager, Lord, to share the good things that you give us.

Grant us such a measure of your Spirit that we may find more joy in giving than in getting.

Make us ready to give cheerfully without grudging, secretly without praise, and in sincerity without looking for gratitude; for Jesus Christ's sake.

John Hunter

Generosity 67

Give me open hands, O God, hands ready to share with all in want the blessings with which you enrich my life.

Deliver me from all meanness and miserliness.

Let me hold my money in stewardship and all my worldly goods in trust for you.

Make me thankful and keep me faithful, for the sake of Jesus Christ my Lord.

John Baillie*

God . . . generously gives us everything for our enjoyment. (1 Timothy 6.17)

Father, how marvellously generous you are to your children!

The benefits you shower upon us every day are more than we can count and far more than we deserve.

For all you give us make us truly grateful; and teach us in turn to be generous not only in our giving but also in our thinking and judging and in all our human relationships; for your goodness and mercy's sake.

Ingratitude 69

Father, in your presence we remember not only your goodness but also our ingratitude.

We have taken your gifts for granted and used them selfishly.

We have thought too much about our own needs, too little about the needs of others.

We have remembered our troubles and forgotten our blessings.

In your mercy forgive us and make us more thankful, for the sake of your Son our Saviour Jesus Christ.

Adapted

Idols 70

My children, keep yourselves from false gods. (1 John 5.21)

The apostle John warned the Christians of his day to keep themselves from idols.

Idolatry was common in the pagan world of his day. It is common still in other forms in our own time:

in the worship of money and possessions,
in the worship of success and fame,
in the worship of pleasure and sport,
in the worship of man instead of the living and true God.

Let us search our own hearts and then pray to the Lord;

> *The dearest idol I have known,*
> *Whate'er that idol be,*
> *Help me to tear it from thy throne,*
> *And worship only thee.*
>
> William Cowper

6

IN TIME OF NEED

In trouble 71

The Lord . . . is their stronghold in time of trouble. (Psalm 37.39)

Our Father, the psalmist knew all about times of trouble. And so do we.

You never promised that our life on earth would be trouble-free.

From time to time we all have our troubles of different kinds: health troubles, family troubles, marriage troubles, business troubles, money troubles, and more.

But the psalmist not only spoke of times of trouble.

He also declared that you were his stronghold at such times.

Lord, be our stronghold too when trouble comes.

I said: 72

    Lord, why should this happen to me?
    What did I do to deserve it?
    How can I possibly cope?

He said:

    Don't blame me; cling to me.
    Don't question me; trust me.
    Don't shut me out; call me in.

      You are not alone;
      I am with you now;
      rest in my love.

Source unknown

Our Father, hear us as we remember in the quietness of our
hearts those we love who are ill.

We name them before you one by one . . .

You love them and know their needs far better than we
do.

We do not dictate to you.

All we ask is that you will do for them as you see best,
and bless them with your peace; for the sake of our Lord
Jesus Christ.

We pray for all carers,
doctors, nurses and for those concerned
with the future of the NHS after 50 years of its
life

God our Father, 74
you are the source of all health and healing,
    all strength and peace.
Teach us to know you more truly
    and trust you more firmly.
Take from us all that hinders your healing power,
    all anxieties and fears.
And help us in our weakness to rest in your love
    and enter into the stillness of your presence;
through Jesus Christ our Lord.

                                                    Adapted

Patience 75

Lord, teach me the art of patience while I am well, and
give me the use of it while I am sick.

In that day either lighten my burden or strengthen my
back.

So often in my health I have discovered my weakness,
presuming on my own strength.

Make me strong in my sickness when I rely solely on
your aid.

                        Adapted from a 17th century prayer by
                                            Thomas Fuller

Lord Jesus Christ, who for love of our souls entered the deep darkness of the cross:

we pray that your healing love may surround all who are in the darkness of great mental distress and who find it difficult to pray for themselves.

May they know that darkness and light are both alike to you and that you have promised never to fail them or forsake them.

Llewellyn Cumings

77

Heavenly Father, we bring to you in prayer people who are suffering in mind or spirit.

We remember especially those facing long and incurable illness;

those cast down by the cares and sorrows of daily life;

those who have lost their faith and for whom the future is dark.

In your mercy maintain their courage, lift their burdens and renew their faith, that they may find in you their strength, their comfort and their peace; for our Saviour's sake.

Depression 78

Strong Son of God, come to me now and rescue me from this state of despair into which I have fallen.

May I know that you are near me,
that you love me still,
and that your love will never change.

Dispel the gloom of my doubt and depression, and may your peace take possession of my whole being; for your mercy's sake.

79

Lord, in your mercy keep us from falling into despondency of mind or spirit.

Lift us from the dark valley of despair to the bright mountain of hope;

from the midnight of desperation to the daybreak of joy.
Lord, yours is the power; let yours be also the glory.

Adapted from words of Martin Luther King

Fear 80

Though I walk through the darkest valley, I will fear no evil, for you are with me. (Psalm 23.4)

Lord, your servant David had nothing to fear because he knew that you were by his side.

For us too life has its dark valleys when fears threaten our peace:

fears about our health and our future,
fears about our work and our money,
fears about our later years and our death.

At such times, O Lord, may the light of your presence dispel our darkness, banish our fears, and restore peace to our hearts.

The handicapped 81

So many people, Lord, and people known to us, are handicapped and unable to live a normal life.

We think of the blind and deaf, the physically afflicted and mentally ill, and especially the victims of incurable disease.

We ask you to give them great patience and perseverance; to surround them with good friends ready to help; and to make them know that your love for them is so strong that it will hold them fast to the end.

33

The blind

Heavenly Father, those of us who have the gift of sight cannot imagine what life would be like without it.

So with deep sympathy we pray for the blind and partially blind.

Give grace also to those who share their daily life and minister to their needs; and while they live in physical darkness, grant them the inner light of the Spirit to discern those things which the human eye cannot see, and the courage to wait patiently until at last they enter your presence and see you face to face; through Christ our Lord.

The lonely

Loving Father, we bring to you those who specially need our prayers, and yet more your presence, in their loneliness; the elderly, the sick, the handicapped, the housebound.

Save us from being so wrapped up in our own concerns that we forget them, and so busy that we fail to bring them what help and comfort we can.

You have given so much to us. Make us sensitive to the needs of others, for Jesus' sake.

The aged

Look with mercy, heavenly Father, on those whose increasing years bring them weakness, distress, or isolation.

Provide for them homes of dignity and peace;

give them understanding helpers, and the willingness to accept help;

and as their strength diminishes, increase their faith and their assurance of your love.

This we ask in the name of Jesus Christ our Lord.

Episcopal Church in the USA

Lord Jesus Christ, we thank you that in sharing our life on earth you also entered into the experience of our death and what follows.

As we trust you with our life, so we may surely trust you also with our death.

When that time comes, give us in your mercy a peaceful end free from fear, knowing that you are with us and that at the last we shall be with you in our Father's house for evermore.

Those who have died   86

We give back to you, O God, those whom you gave to us.

You did not lose them in giving them to us, and we do not lose them by their return to you.

So death is only a horizon, and a horizon is only the limit of our sight.

Open our eyes to see this more clearly, and draw us closer to you, that we may know we are then nearer to our loved ones who are with you, the Lord of life and death.

After William Penn, 1644–1718

Bereavement   87

My Father, help me at this time to remember that you know the sorrows of my heart; that you are not far from me but always close at hand, sharing my burden and entering into my grief.

Teach me in simple trust to rest on your unchanging love and find courage and strength for each day as it comes; for Jesus' sake.

PART TWO

The Christian Pilgrimage

1

PRAISE AND THANKSGIVING

An endless Alleluia   88

'*Alleluia! sing to Jesus*', says the hymn.
Alleluia is my song today:

    Alleluia for Jesus himself,
    Alleluia for his redeeming love,
    Alleluia for his resurrection glory,
    Alleluia for his heavenly reign,
    Alleluia for his body the Church,
    Alleluia for his gift of eternal life.

There is nowhere I can stop with my Alleluias!
Lord, let my life be an endless Alleluia to your glory.

All praise   89

Lord Jesus Christ, Saviour of the world,

    we praise you for loving us all;
    we praise you for dying for us all;
    we praise you for rising triumphant for us all;
    we praise you for interceding in heaven for us all;
    we praise you for giving the Holy Spirit to us all.

All this for us all!
Let us all praise you and magnify you for ever.

God alone is good

Let us ascribe all that is good
to the most high and supreme Lord God
and thank him for everything,
he from whom all good things come.
And may he, who alone is true God,
receive from us and every creature
all honour, praise, dominion and glory;
for every good is his,
and he alone is good.

Adapted from St Francis

God made us for himself 91

O Lord, you are great and highly to be praised.
   Great is your power, and your wisdom has no limits.
   And we men and women, a tiny part of your great work
of creation, want to celebrate your praise.
   It is you who have awakened this desire in us, since you
made us for yourself and our hearts can find no peace until
they rest in you.

Adapted from St Augustine

How great thou art! 92

Great is the Lord and highly to be praised! (Psalm 48.1)

We acknowledge your greatness, O Lord.
   You are the everlasting God, the mighty Creator,

the King of the universe, supreme over all.
   May the thought of your greatness enter deeply into our
hearts,

   to enlarge our vision of you,
   to enrich our worship of you,
   to increase our faith in you.

   You are great indeed, O Lord, and highly to be praised –
by us and by all creation.

Praise for the incarnate Christ 93

All praise and honour to you, Lord Jesus,
the eternal Word who took our flesh
and became man for our salvation.
All praise for your birth and humiliation;
all praise for sharing our human life and limitations;
all praise for entering into our sufferings and trials;
all praise for identifying yourself with our sins
and dying for us on the cross.
Jesus, Saviour, Redeemer, true God and true Man,
we glorify you for ever.

Praise for the Living Christ 94

We give you praise, our Father, that Christ is alive, the
conqueror of all his foes and ours.
   We thank you for his risen presence and power in our
lives from day to day.
   We thank you that he has overcome death and opened
the gate of everlasting life to all who believe.
   Accept our praise, and keep us rejoicing in the faith of
him who died for us and is alive for evermore.

We praise you, Lord Christ,
  because you have ascended up on high
and now reign on the throne of the universe,
  crowned with glory and honour.
We acknowledge your kingship,
  we worship and adore you.
Accept the homage we offer,
  come and reign over us,
and extend your empire over all the world,
  to the glory of God the Father.

Thanksgiving for creation 96

We thank you, O Lord, for what we see of your creation.
  We see the earth and the sky and the light which was
separated from the darkness.
  We see the firmament of heaven and the vast expanse of
the universe.
  We see the lights of heaven aglow, the sun by day, the
moon and the stars by night.
  We see the beauty of the waters gathered up in vast
oceans, and the dry land giving birth to grass and trees.
  We see man made in your image, thus possessing
intelligence and ruling over all unintelligent life.
  And as we see these things, we see also that they are all
very good, and give you thanks.

Adapted from St Augustine

Praise for the Word of God 97

Almighty Father, we praise you for your word:
  for your creative word in the beginning, when you spoke
and the universe came into being;

for the written word, the word of truth enshrined in the
scriptures, by which we are made wise for salvation;

most of all we praise you for Jesus the living Word, the
Word made flesh, who revealed you to us and reconciled
us to you.

All glory to your name.

Thanksgiving for those who have died 98

We give you thanks, our God and Father,
for all those who have died in the faith of Christ;
for the memory of their words and deeds
    and all they accomplished in their time;
for the joyful hope of reunion with them
    in the world to come;
and for our communion with them now in your Son,
    Jesus Christ our Lord.

Source unknown

2

CHRISTIAN DISCIPLESHIP

The new Christian 99

Lord, it is wonderful to be a Christian!
It is wonderful to know that you love me and have forgiven my sins and are always close beside me.
Thank you, Lord. Thank you for all this.
Help me now to go further in this new life:

to grow in grace and strength,
to know and love you better,
and to serve you all my days
in the fellowship of your Church.

Make me what you want me to be and keep me faithful to the end.

Conversion 100

O happy day that fixed my choice
On thee, my Saviour and my God!
Well may this glowing heart rejoice,
And tell its raptures all abroad.

'Tis done, the great transaction's done!
I am my Lord's and he is mine;
He drew me and I followed on,
Charmed to confess the voice divine.

Phillip Doddridge 1702–51

Heavenly Father, we confess how often we disobey
    what we know to be your will;
how often we forget you
    and leave you out of our lives;
how often we are too blind to know our sins,
    too proud to admit them,
    too indifferent to make amends.
We confess how half-hearted we are
    as members of your Church
    and as your witnesses before other people.
In your mercy, O Lord, forgive us our sins,
    and give us humble and penitent hearts,
for the sake of our Saviour Jesus Christ.

After William Temple

A penitent's prayer 102

Lord Jesus Christ,
    I admit that I am a sinner.
I confess my sins to you,
    especially those upon my conscience.
I firmly believe that you died for me
    to bear away my sins.
And now, according to your promise,
    I open my heart to you.
Come in, Lord Jesus,
    and be my Saviour and Friend for ever.

Source unknown

Lord Jesus, give us true faith:

> the faith of the heart and not merely of the intellect;
> the faith that trusts you alone for salvation and not our own merits;
> the faith that shows itself in life and conduct and not simply in religious forms;
> the faith that is strong enough to hold you fast in bad times and not only in good.

Lord, grant us this faith, and strengthen and increase it continually, to your glory.

Forgiveness 104

Heavenly Father, you have taught us by your Son that if we do not forgive others we cannot receive your forgiveness.

Make us merciful in our dealings with those who do us wrong, as we recall how mercifully you have dealt with us; that forgiven much, we may forgive much, for the sake of him who died that we might be forgiven, our Saviour Jesus Christ.

Love 105

Lord, teach us the true meaning of love and also give us grace to practise it, for if we have no love we are nothing.

> Love is patient and kind and envies no one.
> Love is never boastful or conceited or rude.
> Love is never selfish or quick to take offence.
> Love does not rejoice in wrong but rejoices in right.
> Love is always eager to believe the best, always
>   hopeful, always patient.
> Love is eternal, for love is God and God is Love.

Based on 1 Corinthians 13.3-8

Lord God, you have called us to be doers of the word and not hearers only.

Help us to remember that what you require of your servants is not profession but practice, not words but deeds.

May we honestly measure the quality of our lives by the one thing that matters: obedience to your word.

Humility 107

We worship you, Lord Christ, because for our sake
 you emptied yourself of your power and glory
and clothed yourself in our humanity,
 to live in poverty on earth
 and suffer the shame of death on the cross.
Teach us the lesson of your humility
 and empty our lives of all pride,
 all selfish ideas and ambitions;
that we too may take the form of a servant
 and find fulfilment in doing the Father's will.

Based on Philippians 2.5–8

Holiness 108

God our Father, deliver us from the power of sin
 and sanctify us by your Holy Spirit.
Draw us nearer to the Lord Jesus Christ,
 and deepen our fellowship with him,
that we may become daily more like him
 and reflect the beauty of his holiness in our lives,
for your greater glory.

Lord, you have called us to holiness.

Keep us in purity of thought and deed, and help us to honour you in our bodies as well as in our spirits.

May we never forget that we have been bought at a price; that in the totality of our being we belong to you and that our body is the shrine of the indwelling Holy Spirit.

Accept us, O Lord, as we offer our whole selves to you, a living sacrifice, and make us fit instruments for your service, to your greater glory.

Based on 1 Thessalonians 4.7; 1 Corinthians 6.19,20; and Romans 12.1

Fellowship in Christ 110

Heavenly Father, in the Church of your Son you have made us members one of another, so that we belong to each other and are called to love and serve each other.

Deepen our sense of fellowship in Christ.

Help us remember that though we differ in certain ways and do not all think alike, we are all equally members of your family on earth, as we shall be in heaven.

Nothing will separate us then. May nothing separate us now, for our Lord's sake.

111

Bind us together, Lord, and make us one body in Christ.

Break down the divisions between believers.

Help us to forget our differences and put aside our prejudices; so that the people of your pilgrim Church, led by the Spirit towards your kingdom, may work, pray and live happily together in charity and in peace.

*The Catholic Prayer Book**

The life of service — a personal reflection

God has created me to do him some definite service.

He has given some work to me which he has not given to another.

I have my mission. I may never know it in this life, but I shall be told it in the next.

He has not created me for nothing.

Therefore I will trust him. Whatever, wherever I am, I can never be thrown away.

He does nothing in vain.

He knows what he is about.

Adapted from words of John Henry Newman

Our witness 113

Lord God, as those who seek to be your witnesses in a minority situation, where your claims are so largely ignored or denied, we pray that we may bear our Christian witness by what we are and not simply by what we profess or preach.

Give us true holiness of character,
a deeper understanding of people and their needs,
and a love that is humble, outgoing and open.

So may our lives reflect something of your grace made known to us in Jesus Christ our Lord.

Based on words of George Appleton

The presence of Christ 114

Lord Jesus Christ, you have promised to be with us always, to the end of time.

Help us to be so conscious of your presence in our daily lives that we may be kept in peace of mind and free from all fear or anxiety; and in your presence may we find fullness of joy and strength to persevere, to the glory of God the Father.

Life's battle 115

Our Father, you have called us to be good soldiers of Jesus Christ and to fight valiantly under his banner.

In the battle of life give us grace to contend fearlessly for truth, goodness and justice, and to oppose evil whatever form it takes and wherever it is to be found.

In all things make us more than conquerors through him who loves us, our Lord and Saviour Jesus Christ.

The Christian hope 116

Lord Jesus Christ, we praise you that for those who put their trust in you death is not a leap in the dark but a joyous homecoming.

We thank you for the heavenly home which you have gone to prepare for us.

Prepare us also for that home; and in your mercy bring us at last to be partakers of its joys and to dwell with you for evermore.

117

All praise to the God and Father of our Lord Jesus Christ!

In his great mercy we have been born anew and given a living hope by the resurrection of Jesus Christ from the dead.

And the heavenly inheritance that awaits us as his children is one that is imperishable, unfading and undefiled.

It is reserved in heaven for us who through faith are guarded by God's power until the salvation that is to be revealed at the end of time.

From 1 Peter 1.3–5

Heavenly Father, save us from thinking of prayer as difficult or burdensome.

You have planted in every heart the instinct to pray, and true prayer is simply holding communion with you, in any way, in any place, at any time.

So teach us to pray openly, trustfully, confidently, unselfishly, remembering the needs of others as well as our own, and giving thanks always in the name of our Lord Jesus Christ.

Listening 119

Father, when I speak to you in prayer
I must not do all the talking.
I must give you a chance to speak to me
as we hold communion with one another.
In the quietness of your presence
may I hear your still small voice and reply,
'Speak Lord, your servant is listening.'

Worship 120

I was glad when they said unto me:
'Let us go to the house of the Lord.' (Psalm 122.1)

Father, may it be our delight as well as our duty
  to worship you in the fellowship of the Church.
Prepare us in mind and spirit for our worship
  and tune our hearts to sing your praise.
May we receive all that you have to give us
  and offer all that you require of us;
and may we carry the spirit of worship
  into our daily life and work;
through Jesus Christ our Lord.

We thank you, heavenly Father, for Sunday.

We thank you because it is our Christian Sabbath, the day of rest, when we lay aside our daily work, relax our minds and bodies, and gain refreshment of spirit.

We thank you still more because Sunday is our celebration of Easter, the day of resurrection, when we celebrate our risen Lord's triumph on the first day of the week and meet him in worship with his Church throughout the world.

Let Sunday always be for us a special day, a joyful day, the best day of the week.

3

DEVOTIONAL PRAYERS

Love for God   122

Heavenly Father, we love you
  because you first loved us.
Yet our love for you is so feeble
  while your love for us is so strong.
Teach us more of your love,
  that we may love you better;
and help us to show our love for you
  by our love for others.

Based on 1 John 4.19

Loving and giving   123

God so loved the world that he gave his only Son . . .
(John 3.16)

Our Father, in those words we find the key to all our
love and all our giving.

We love – because you first loved us.
We give – because you first gave to us.

True love always gives, and gives unselfishly and sacrifi-
cially.

Teach us to love and give like that; and all glory be to
your name.

Lord Jesus, you know everything:
  you know that I love you.
How could it be otherwise?
  For it was you who first loved me,
  the unlovely and unlovable,
and died for me, pardoned me
  and welcomed me into your family.
Lord, you know everything:
  you know that I love you.

Friend of sinners 125

Lord Jesus, friend of sinners,
  be a friend to me.
For I know I am a sinner
  and need your love and friendship.
Lord Jesus, be my friend today
  and all my days.

Lord Jesus, my friend, **126**
you love me and know all about me.
You understand my deepest needs
and have forgiven all my sins.
Teach me to love you more,
and how to love other people
in the way you love me.

Bible Society*

Lord, help me to trust you wholly,
for you yourself are the answer to all my need:

> my help in trouble,
> my refuge in danger,
> my strength in temptation,
> my comfort in sorrow,
> my guide in uncertainty,
> my hope in despondency,

my God, now and for evermore.

Lord, you are our God and we are your people: 128

> you are our Maker and we are your creatures;
> you are our King and we are your subjects;
> you are our Shepherd and we are your flock;
> you are our Father and we are your children.

Glory to your name!

> Based on a Jewish prayer

Father, save us from all needless anxiety 129
and help us to entrust

> the past to your mercy,
> the present to your love,
> and the future to your wisdom,

in the name of Jesus Christ our Lord.

For grace

Loving Father, may I know the poverty of my spirit,
    that I may be rich in your grace.
May I be truly sorry for my sin,
    that I may receive your forgiveness.
May I hunger and thirst for the truth,
    that I may rejoice in your word.

After Jeremy Taylor

Most gracious God, give to us and to all your people:

    in times of anxiety, serenity;
    in times of hardship, courage;
    in times of uncertainty, patience;

and at all times a quiet trust in your fatherly love and
wisdom; for Jesus' sake.

For peace

Lord Jesus Christ, you know the restlessness of our hearts.
    Make your promised gift of peace a reality in our lives,
that everything we undertake may be done without worry
or fuss.
    In all our fears and anxieties help us to rest on your help
and to find calmness in the knowledge that you are always
by our side, our loving Saviour and Friend.

We cannot as Christians pray for peace at any price, but
only for the right kind of peace.

> Show us, good Lord,
>   the peace we should seek,
>   the peace we must give,
>   the peace we can keep,
>   the peace we must forgo,
>   and the peace you have given us
> in Jesus Christ our Lord.

Source unknown

True happiness 134

O Lord, take away from my mind the idea that *any* joy
whatsoever is happiness.

There is one joy that is not granted to the ungodly but
only to those who give you honour, without expecting any
reward.

For them, you yourself are joy.

This indeed is happiness: rejoicing in you, rejoicing
about you, and rejoicing for you – this and nothing else.

Whoever believes that there is happiness other than in
you is pursuing something different, not the possession of
true happiness.

After St Augustine

Fill thou my life, O Lord my God,
In every part with praise.

We acknowledge, our Father, that there is often praise on
our lips but not much in our hearts, still less in our lives.

Forgive us in your mercy and restore to us the joy of your
salvation.

Fill our life in every part with praise, that we may carry
the spirit of praise into everything we do.

So shalt thou, Lord, receive from me
The praise and glory due;
And so shall I begin on earth
The song for ever new.

Based on a hymn of Horatius Bonar, 1808–89

Lord, what can you make of me?   136

I am only a spark. Make me a fire.
I am only a string. Make me a lyre.
I am only a drop. Make me a fountain.
I am only an ant-hill. Make me a mountain.
I am only a feather. Make me a wing.
I am only a rag. Make me a king!

A prayer from Mexico

All things new   137

Lord God, creator of the world, we rejoice that you can
make all things new.

Give us grace to trust you daily for fresh love and in-
spiration, fresh courage and perseverance.

Make us always ready to see the new ways you show us

and to follow you in whichever direction you lead.

May the Lord Jesus himself ever be new to us, and so may our love for him.

Church Missionary Society*

Pilgrims 138

Heavenly Father, you have taught us that our life on earth is a pilgrimage from this world to that which is to come.

Guide us on our journey; defend us from the perils of the way; and save us from going astray into by-path meadow.

May ours be a pilgrim's progress; and as we press on our way may it be with a song of praise in our hearts; and by your grace may we endure faithfully till we reach the celestial City and receive your welcome home.

Based on John Bunyan's *Pilgrim's Progress*

Others 139

Lord, when I am hungry
    give me someone to feed;
when I am thirsty
    give water for their thirst;
when I am sad
    give me someone to lift from sorrow;
when I am weighed down,
    lay on my shoulders the burden of others.
May your will be my bread,
    your grace my strength,
    your love my resting-place.

Translated from the French *Prayers of Faith*

Lord Jesus, you stand at my door and knock.
   You will not force your way in.
   You respect my freedom and await my response.
   May the door of my heart always be open to you and
may every room in my life which you would enter be
prepared and ready to welcome you, my Saviour, my
Master, and my God.

                                        Based on Revelation 3.20

Insight   141

Lord God, as you have given me the gift of sight, I pray
that I may see not only with the eyes of my head but with
the eyes of my heart also; that I may perceive the beauty
and meaning of all I behold and glorify you, the Creator of
all, blessed for evermore.

                                        George Appleton

Dedication   142

Lord, take me as I am
with all my faults and failures
and make me what you want me to be.
I give myself to you, my whole self,
   my gifts and talents,
   my health and intellect,
   and all my future days,
that you may fulfil in me and through me
your purpose for my life in the world,
   for your great glory.

4

SHORT PRAYERS

Priorities
143

Teach us, Lord, to put the needs of others before our own,
  our duty before our pleasure,
   the things of the Spirit before the things of the
    body,
  and above all to put you before everything else.

Self-knowledge
144

O God, the searcher of hearts, help us to see ourselves in
the light of your holiness; that we may hate and turn from
our sins, receive your grace and forgiveness, and learn to
love and serve you better; for Jesus' sake.

In his steps
145

Lord Jesus Christ, help us to follow more closely in your
footsteps; that we may manifest in our own lives the
compassion and understanding you have shown us in
yours; for your honour and glory.

Filled with the Spirit
146

Heavenly Father, empty us of self and fill us with your
Holy Spirit; that we may produce in abundance the fruits
of love, joy and peace, and glorify you in lives hallowed by
your presence in our hearts.

Fidelity

My God and Father, let me never be shaken
  in my faithfulness towards you,
  in my strictness towards myself,
  and in my charity towards others.

God's will

For light to know your will,
for courage to obey your will,
for a heart to love your will,
    we pray, our Father, in Christ's name.

The unchanging one

Lord, you are unchanging: not only in your love for us and
in your purpose for our lives, but unchanging also in your
claim upon our love, our obedience and our service.

Peace

Lord Jesus, grant us your promised gift of peace: your own
peace such as the world cannot give and can never take
away; that our hearts may be untroubled and our lives be
free from fear.

Based on John 14.27

Grace

God of all grace, in asking your forgiveness
I can claim no right to be forgiven
or plead any merit of my own,
but simply cast myself on your unbounded love.

Profession and practice

Father, we pray that we who profess to be Christians may
also practise our faith and allow our creed to speak
through our life; that others may catch some glimpse of
your love and give you the glory.

Help us, good Lord, so that we who are among the people
who most frequently speak your name may also be those
who most readily do your will.

Being and becoming

Heavenly Father, give us grace to accept what we are,
with all our faults and limitations; and yet more grace to
become what you want us to be in the power of the Spirit
of our Lord Jesus Christ.

A twofold blessing

My Father and my God, in your goodness grant me this
twofold blessing:
  the grace to forget myself
    and all my failure;
  and the grace never to forget you
    and all your love.

PART THREE

The World We Live In

1
CREATION

The Creator 156

Almighty God, from everlasting to everlasting the same, we worship and adore you.

You are the maker of all things visible and invisible: heaven and earth are full of the majesty of your glory.

We bless you for your wisdom, power and love made manifest in your works, and with all creation we join in praising you, the glorious and ever-living God, for ever and ever.

Source unknown

Our creation 157

Almighty God, maker of heaven and earth, we praise you for the world you have made to be our home and for everything you have given us so richly to enjoy.

We praise you too for our own creation as men and women made in your image,

with minds to know you,
hearts to love you,
and wills to obey you.

Accept our gratitude and may our lives from day to day show forth your glory.

Reverence for creation 158

Show us, O God, how to love not only animals, birds, and all green and growing things, but the soil, air and water by

which we live, so that we may not exploit or pollute them
for our own profit or convenience.

Help us to cherish these necessities for our survival; and
guide those in authority to ensure that the human spirit
may not be starved in pursuit of material comfort and
wealth.

Phoebe Hesketh

159

Help us, O Lord our God, to see in the beauty of the world
around us the reflection of your eternal glory.

Open our eyes to all the signs of your love, and enable us
so to live that we may hold all created things in reverence
for your sake who made them all; through Jesus Christ our
Lord.

Source unknown

The good earth　160

Almighty God, Lord of all creation, we thank you for the
mystery of life and growth;
　for the good earth we plough and sow and cultivate,
　and for the food it yields for the life of mankind.

May we show our gratitude by our efforts to conserve
the vitality of the soil and by our concern for a fair dis-
tribution of the earth's resources; for the sake of Jesus
Christ our Lord.

Adapted

Earth's beauty　161

Lord, while there is so much marvellous beauty in the
world you made for us to live in and to enjoy, we confess
with shame that we litter it with so many sordid and ugly
things of our own making.

Dear Father, forgive our foolish ways and reclothe us in

our rightful minds, that we may have a better understanding of creation and a deeper reverence for the work of your hands.

The Canticle of the Sun162

Almighty Lord God, all praise, glory, honour and blessing be yours for ever!

Praise be to my Lord God for all his works, and especially for our brother the sun, who brings us the light of day and shines on us with great splendour.

Praised be my Lord for our sister the moon and for the stars which he has set clear and lovely in the heavens.

Praised be my Lord for our brother the wind and for all weather by which he sustains the life of his creatures.

Praised be my Lord for our sister water, who is very serviceable to us and humble and precious and clean.

Praised be my Lord for our mother the earth who nourishes us and brings forth many kinds of fruit and gives us the green grass and the flowers.

Praise and bless the Lord and give him thanks, and serve him with great humility.

Abridged version of the Song of St Francis

Harvest163

We thank you, our Father, that you so faithfully fulfil your promise to mankind, that seed time and harvest shall not fail.

We thank you for the fruits of the earth in their season, for the harvest of the seas and for the food brought to us from other lands.

Give us always thankful hearts for these your gifts, and may we who have plenty remember others who have little, for Jesus Christ's sake.

Almighty Father, we thank you for the amazing variety of life in your world and especially for the changing seasons.

We thank you for the spring with its vitality and freshness and with all nature breaking out into life in harmony with Easter.

We thank you for the summer with its sunshine and long warm days and the flowers in their abundance and beauty.

We thank you for the autumn with its mellow fruitfulness, for the gifts of harvest and the glowing colours of the trees.

We thank you for the winter with its cold dark days, the snow and the ice and the warmth of Christmas.

Changing are the seasons, our God, but unchanging are your goodness and our gratitude, in Christ Jesus our Lord.

Animals   165

Heavenly Father, in your love you have made every living creature on earth.

Teach us to show kindness to all animals and save us from inflicting pain on any of them, for you made them as well as us and entrusted them to our care.

Make us merciful in all our dealings, even as you have been merciful to us in Christ.

Birds   166

Almighty God, we rejoice that you who made us in your image made also the eagle and the sparrow and all winged creatures.

We thank you for the varied beauty of the birds and

their songs and for all the pleasure they give us.

Help us to show our gratitude by caring for this marvellous part of your creation, for the honour of your name.

Marlborough College*

The world and ourselves 167

Our Father, as we think of the marvels of the world around us, help us to think even more of you, who made it all, and to worship only the Creator, not the created.

Help us also to treasure and guard the world's rich resources and to share its wealth with the impoverished nations, that none may die of hunger when so much food abounds; for the sake of Christ our Lord.

2

WORLD ISSUES

Our world   168

Lord God, we are sometimes frightened by the state of our
world with its naked wickedness, its ruthless cruelty, its
wanton disregard for human life.

This is not the world you intended for man your creature, made in your likeness, made for your glory and for
his good.

Lord, have mercy on our lost world and on sinful, rebel-
lious mankind.

You have shown us in Jesus Christ your way of peace.

Forgive our folly and bring us to our senses, that we may
follow your way and abandon our own.

World peace   169

Father, we all long for the peace of the world, but we are
so slow to learn what all history teaches us, that there can
be no peace without justice and no justice without godliness.

Help us to see that peace is the fruit of righteousness and
that righteousness is founded on faith: faith in you the
living God and your redeeming, transforming love.

In our search for peace may we get our priorities right,
that our quest may not be in vain.

                                                170
Lord of our world, we acknowledge with shame and sor-
row all the sin, hatred and injustice which have led and
still lead to violence and war.

Grant us your forgiveness and your peace.

It is the peace which the world cannot give but which we could give to the world.

Lord, give us grace to be peacemakers, in the name of Jesus, the Prince of peace.

Pauline Bower*

World leaders 171

Sovereign Lord of men and nations, we pray for rulers and statesmen who are called to leadership in the affairs of the world.

Give them vision to see far into the issues of their time,
courage to uphold what they believe to be right,
and integrity in their words and motives.

And may their service to their people promote the welfare and peace of all mankind; through Jesus Christ our Lord.

Basil Naylor

World poverty 172

Lord, we all know that while we in this country have an abundance of good things, much of the world is in terrible want;

while we have money enough and to spare,
vast numbers are desperately poor;
while we have far more to eat than we need,
multitudes are dying of starvation.

Lord, give us the courage to face these things and to think more deeply about them; and may thought lead to action in whatever way is in our power; for the sake of Jesus who we confess to be our Lord.

Lord Jesus, you looked with compassion on the hungry people of your day and fed them.

Hear us as we pray in your name for the starving and dying multitudes of our own time.

Show us, who have so much, what we can do to help those who have so little; and prosper the efforts of all engaged in planning and sending relief, that out of the world's vast bounty the needs of all may be supplied.

The suffering world 174

God of love and Father of us all, we know that sin always leads to suffering.

Have mercy on those who are suffering in our world today as the result of war and civil strife:

the wounded and handicapped,
the dying and bereaved,
the homeless and impoverished,
the starving and refugees.

Bless the agents of righteousness and reconciliation at work among the stricken nations, and give peace in our time; for the sake of our Saviour Jesus Christ.

Adapted

The world's evil 175

God our Father, deliver us from evil: not only the evil in our own hearts but the evil in our world today:

the evil of unjust governments and tyrannical regimes;
the evil of religious intolerance and racial strife;

the evil of war and the slaughter of countless innocent
lives;
The evil of organised crime, terrorism, and drug traffick-
ing;
the evil of world poverty in a world of abundant wealth.

Deliver us, O God, from all such evil; and let your
kingdom come and your will be done on earth, for the
glory of your name.

God's will for mankind 176

Your will be done on earth.
Father, how often we say those words with an air of
resignation, as though your will were something to be
endured, not enjoyed; a burden, not a blessing.
But your will is all that is for the welfare of mankind.
Your will is justice and peace, health and happiness, life
abundant and freedom for all.
So we pray that your will may be done *on earth*, this
earth, and be done *now*.
Nothing could be better for each one of us and for our
world than that.

A free world 177

Lord God, when so much of the world is in bondage to the
forces of evil and the tyranny of misrule, we pray that all
nations may enjoy the freedom which is their right:

freedom from war and want,
freedom of thought and speech,
freedom to believe and worship according to conscience.

And may we, who now enjoy these privileges, jealously
guard and preserve our freedom for the generations to
come.

We thank you, our Father, that as Christian believers we are part of your worldwide family of the Church and that all its members of every race are our brothers and sisters in Christ.

In that faith we pray for the Church in every land, that it may be true to its Lord:

by preaching the gospel of salvation,
by serving the poor and needy,
by defending the persecuted and oppressed,
and by upholding the cause of justice and freedom.

So may the Church be a visible witness to your grace and an agent of your kingdom in all the world; and the glory be yours for ever.

At this time, we remember especially the Anglican Communion & commend to you the meeting of the Bishops at the Lambeth Conference later this month

The unbelieving world   179

Heavenly Father, your love is so vast that it embraces the whole of mankind and longs for all people to believe in your Son Jesus Christ.

But *how can they believe in one of whom they have not heard?*

We pray therefore that your Church may send more and more messengers to the unbelieving world, to tell others of Christ and of your boundless love for all.

For *how shall they hear without a preacher?*

Based on Romans 10.14

Heavenly Father, help us to remember that your boundless love enfolds all people without distinction;

that every religion is an attempt to know you and respond to you;
that the yearnings of other hearts are much like our own and are known to you.

Give us a clearer understanding of these things; that while we hold fast to our own faith in Christ, we may truly love and serve our neighbour, whatever his religion or race; and this we pray through Jesus our Lord.

Source unknown

World vision 181

God and Father of us all, we confess the narrowness of our vision which so often prevents us from entering into your purpose for the world:

the pride which makes us unwilling to receive the insights of others;
the selfishness which allows us to take our affluence for granted in a world of need and hunger;
the fear which holds us back when we could act.

Father, forgive us. Increase our love for our fellow human beings, and help us to show it in our service of Christ our Lord.

Inter-diocesan West Africa Link*

NATION AND SOCIETY

The nation 182

Lord of our life and God of our salvation, we thank you for our country and all that we owe to it.

We pray for a new and better nation in which men and women may strive not only to gain their rights but even more to fulfil their responsibilities.

Give us all a deeper sense of duty, both to you and to one another; and make us remember that in your kingdom greatness is measured in terms not of wealth and power but of faithfulness and service.

183

Lord God, in our prayers for our country we remember especially the men and women who powerfully influence the life of society:

those who fashion our politics,
those who frame and administer our laws,
those who mould public opinion through the press, radio and television.
those who write what many read.

May all such recognise their responsibility to you and to the nation, that people may be influenced for what is good, not evil; for what is true, not false; for the glory of your name.

Most merciful God, we ask for our nation
   not material prosperity
   or a higher standard of living,
but what is most for its true welfare:

   a renewal of Christian faith,
   a recovery of spiritual values,
   a return to the paths of righteousness;

and this we pray in the name of Christ our Lord.

185

Lord God, as a nation we are learning that lawlessness is the result of godlessness.

As a people we have turned our back on your commandments, ignored your claims, and chosen a materialistic, irreligious way of life.

So while public worship declines and the churches become emptier, crime and wickedness increase and the prisons are full to overflowing.

Father, have mercy on us. Revive your work in our land and grant to us as a people true repentance and a living faith in Christ the Lord.

Reverence   **186**

Almighty God, teach our nation the meaning of reverence in this secular age when people hold nothing sacred and deny the sanctity of life itself.

Increase among us true godliness and the spirit of holy fear; for the fear of the Lord is the beginning of wisdom.

And may we hallow your name in our own lives and never take it in vain.

...d our Father, hear us as we pray for those who serve in ...e parliament of our country.

...id them of party spirit and strife;
...elp them to put first things first;
...ve them a right judgment in all their counsels.

...nd grant that they may make it their one concern to ...our your laws and to do the thing that is right, without ...or favour.

Race relations 188

Lord, help us to see in our fellow countrymen of whatever race or culture people like ourselves for whom Christ died.

Save us from racial prejudice. Give us grace to welcome people of different beliefs into our national life, and the humility to receive from them the good things they have to offer.

We ask in the name of Jesus, the Lord and Saviour of us all.

George Appleton

Social justice 189

Heavenly Father, whose Son Jesus Christ cared for the needs of everyone and went about doing good:

grant us the understanding and resolution to create in this country a just social order;

deepen our concern for the poor, the old, the homeless and the suffering;

and use us as servants of your kingdom to carry out your will in our national life.

Adapted

Law and order 190

Almighty God and Father, we bring to you in prayer those responsible for the maintenance of law and order in our land.

We pray for the judges, the magistrates, and the police:

that the innocent may be protected,
evil doers be brought to account,
and the rights of all be defended.

Grant that as a nation we may enjoy the blessing of a just, free and peaceful society; through Jesus Christ our Lord.

Offenders against the law 191

Christ our Lord,
friend of outcasts and sinners,
give to all offenders against the law
true repentance and the knowledge of your love;
and so change their hearts
that they may make a new start in life
and find freedom in your service.

Adapted

The victims of crime

In these days of violent crime we remember before you, our God, the victims of terrorism, hooliganism and muggings.

We pray for the physically injured; for those who have been robbed of their possessions; and the many whose minds are darkened by fear.

Lord, you once suffered at the hands of men.

Look in mercy on those who suffer today, and bring them your healing love and strength, for your name's sake.

Health service

Heavenly Father, we know that what matters most in life is not our money or our age but our health.

So we give you thanks for those who serve the health of the nation:

for the devotion and skills of doctors, surgeons, and nurses;
for the work of scientists engaged in medical research;
for the staffs of hospitals, clinics and hospices.

Prosper all that is being done to heal the sick, to help the disabled and conquer disease; through Jesus Christ our Lord.

Scientific research

Eternal God and Father, you alone are the source of all truth and understanding.

Direct by your Holy Spirit those engaged in scientific research, that as they uncover more of the treasures of wisdom and knowledge, they may further the universal purpose of your love.

In your mercy increasingly bless the partnership between

religion and science, that faith and reason together may serve your will in promoting the welfare of mankind and in the reconciliation of the whole world to you, its maker and redeemer.

Adapted from words of Tom Torrance

Industry 195

Lord God, we ask you to give courage and resolution to those who are striving for peace and goodwill in the industrial life of the nation.

Grant that there may be greater tolerance and co-operation between management and labour.

Remove grievances and misunderstandings, and let justice and equity prevail; that all may strive together in unity of purpose for the common good; through Jesus Christ our Lord.

Industrial unrest 196

Lord God, as we ask for your help and direction in this time of industrial unrest, we pray that all involved may care more for justice than for gain;

that human rights and responsibilities may be equally recognised;

that every employee may get his worth and give his worth;

and above all that a healthier and happier spirit may prevail in our nation.

The unemployed 197

Our Father, in praying for the unemployed we think especially of those who through no fault of their own have lost their jobs and are now searching for other work for the sake of their families.

May they not grow despondent or come to regard themselves as useless.

Help them to employ their skills and gifts in other directions, and to find a measure of fulfilment in the service of the church or community till employment comes their way again.

People in need 198

Our Father, for those in need we make our prayer:

the sick in mind or body;
the blind and the deaf;
the fatherless and the widow;
the sorrowing and the anxious.

In all their troubles and afflictions give them comfort and courage, and your peace in their hearts; through Jesus Christ our Lord.

The handicapped 199

Lord, hear our prayer for those, both young and old, who are called to bear some bodily affliction every day of their life.

May they have the grace to accept the things they cannot change and to face life with a brave faith and cheerful spirit.

And make them to know that in times of trial and frustration they are not alone, for you are near them and will never let them go.

Adapted

Our Father, we hold before you in prayer the many homeless people of our land.

We ask the Holy Spirit to open our eyes and our hearts to
their distress and suffering.

Though we know that much has been done to secure
more and better housing, we also see the continuing
tragedy of homelessness.

Forgive our indifference to the misery around us, and in
your mercy bless and prosper all that is being done to
remedy this evil; for the sake of Jesus Christ our Lord.

Shelter*

INDEX OF PRINCIPAL SUBJECTS

ACKNOWLEDGEMENTS

In addition to the sources mentioned in the ascriptions to individual prayers, the compiler and publishers are pleased to acknowledge details of sources for the following:

61 and **126** are used by permission of The British and Foreign Bible Society.

170 was adapted from a prayer in the Church Missionary Society *Prayer Paper*.

174 was adapted from a prayer by Richard Morgan which originally appeared in the Church Missionary Society *Prayer Paper*.

41 was adapted from a prayer in *CPAS Prayers* (1972) published by the Church Pastoral-Aid Society.

111 is from the *Catholic Prayer Book* by Anthony Bullen, published and copyrighted (1982) by Darton, Longman and Todd Ltd., and is used by permission of the publishers.

64 was adapted from *Daily Prayer* edited by Eric Milner-White and G.W. Briggs (1941) and is used by permission of Oxford University Press.

67 was adapted from *A Diary of Private Prayer* by John Baillie (1936) and is used by permission of Oxford University Press.

163 was used in *Parish Prayers* (1967); **171** and **173** were used in *Contemporary Parish Prayers* (1975); **20, 43, 101, 123, 184** were used in *New Parish Prayers* (1982); all edited by Frank Colquhoun and published by Hodder and Stoughton.

32, 76, 104, 131, 158, 188 were used in *New Every Morning* edited by Frank Colquhoun (1973) and published by BBC Enterprises.